METAL CATS

COLORING BOOK

ALEXANDRA CROCKETT
Illustrations by CHUCK GONZALES

pH powerHouse Books Brooklyn, NY

Die By

SAT FEB 5TH
Behemoth
LED
ZEPPELIN
STAIRWAY TO HEAVEN

AMON AMARTH

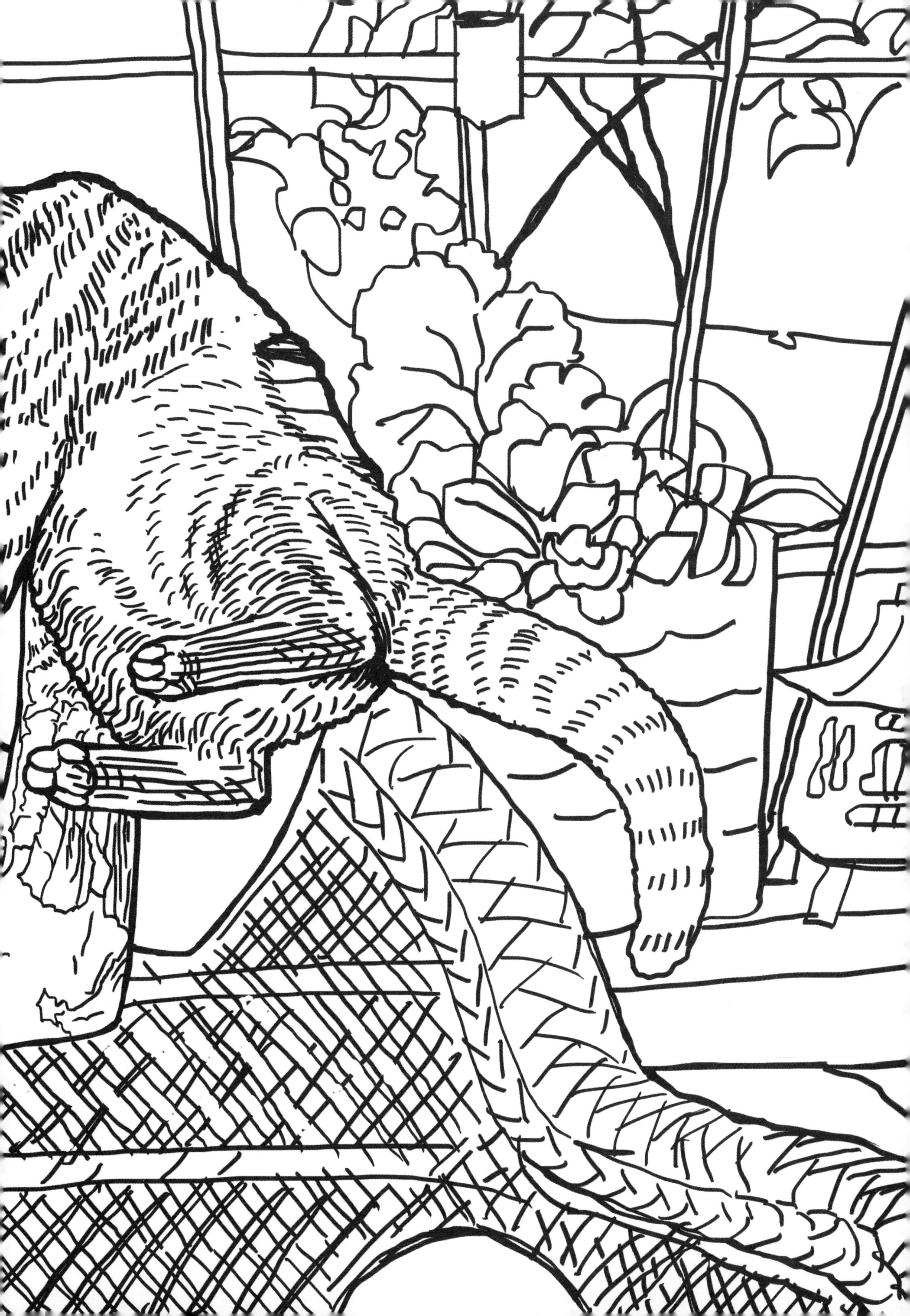

NO

THRASHER
CSS

TAINTED COCAINE, PART II
AND WE
the Stranger
the Stranger
the Stranger

LYMPI
BEER

PIA

FEEL THE FIRE